PIANO • VOCAL • GUITAR

Rick Nowels

COLLECTION

Rick Nowels grew up in the San Franciso Bay area. He has written and produced records in New York, London and Los Angeles, where he currently lives. He can't stop writing songs.

To find out more about Rick go to

www.ricknowels.com

ISBN 0-634-03296-8

HAL•LEONARD®
CORPORATION
7777 W. BLUEMOUND RD. P.O. BOX 13819 MILWAUKEE, WI 53213

Visit Hal Leonard Online at
www.halleonard.com

Rick Nowels

CONTENTS

BODY & SOUL

Words and Music by RICK NOWELS
and ELLEN SHIPLEY

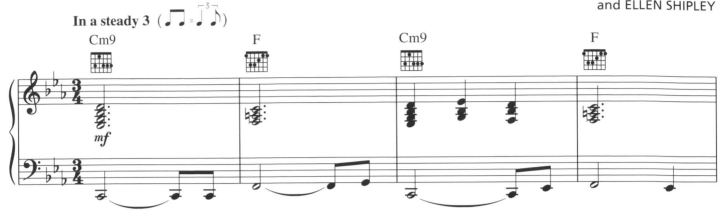

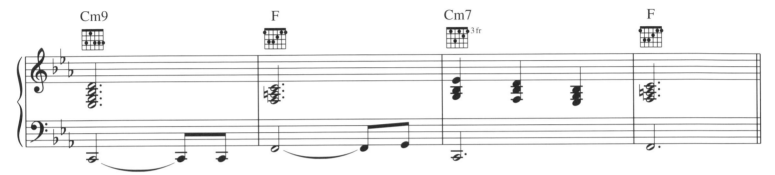

What have you done to me? I can't eat. I
I don't know what to do 'cause all of me wants

can-not sleep and I'm not the same __ an-y-more.
all of you. Do I stand a-lone __ at the shore?

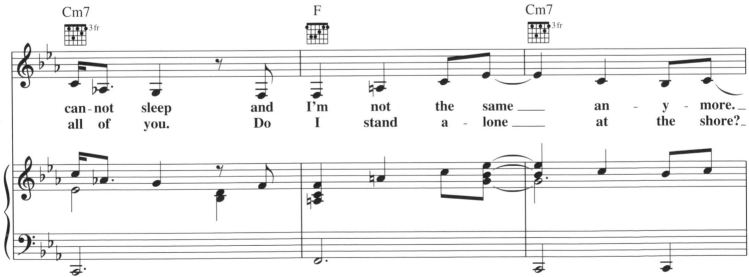

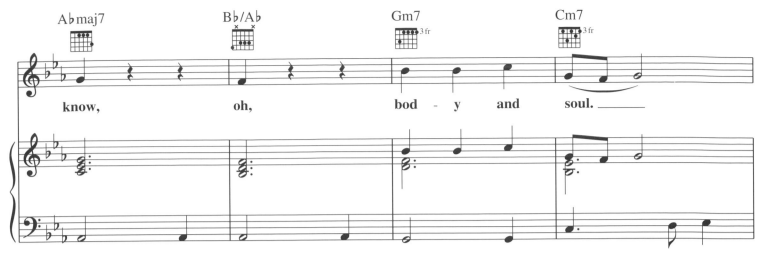

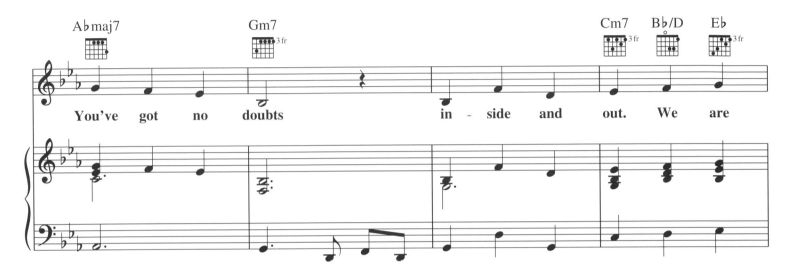

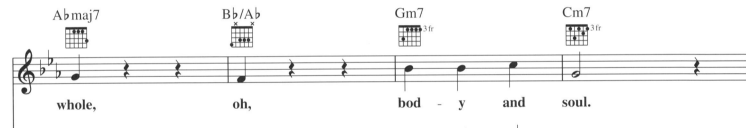

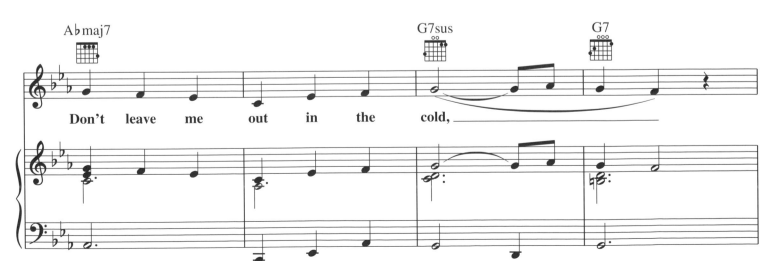

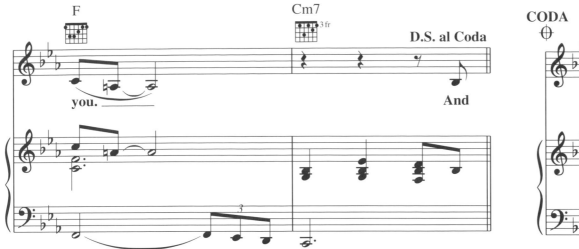

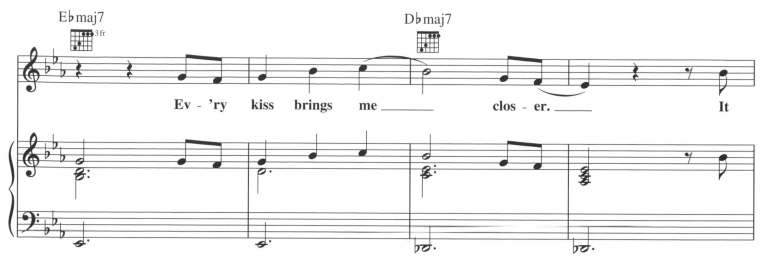

Ev - 'ry kiss brings me _____ clos - er. _____ It

feels _ good to let you in - side. I've got to

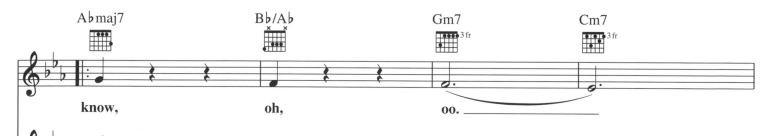

know, oh, oo. _____

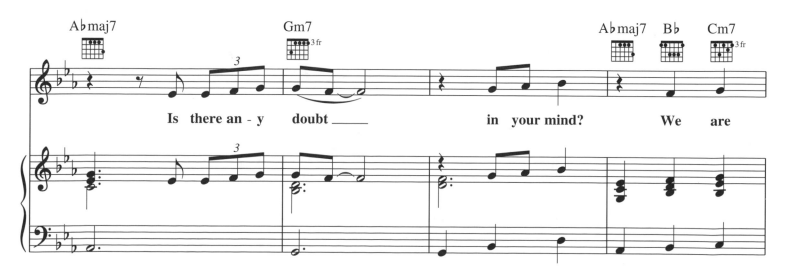

Is there an - y doubt _____ in your mind? We are

FALLING INTO YOU

Words and Music by RICK NOWELS,
MARIE CLAIRE D'UBALDO and BILLY STEINBERG

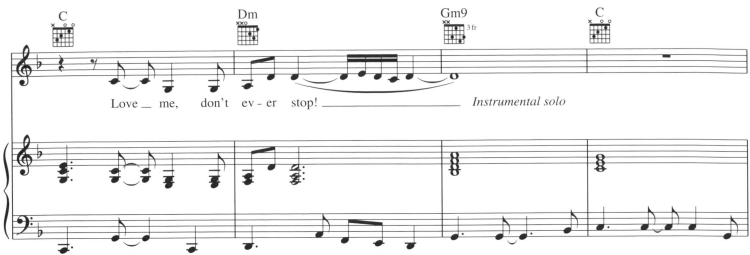

Love __ me, don't ev - er stop! _____ *Instrumental solo*

Solo ends So, close your eyes and let ___ me

kiss you. _____ And while you sleep I will miss __

CIRCLE IN THE SAND

Words and Music by ELLEN SHIPLEY
and RICK NOWELS

THE GAME OF LOVE

Words and Music by RICK NOWELS
and GREGG ALEXANDER

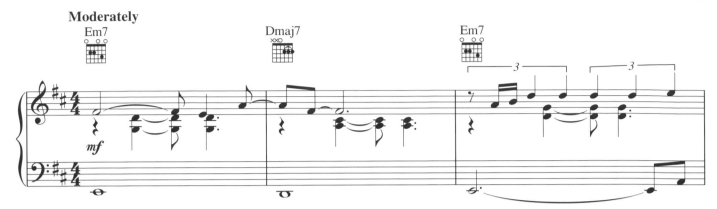

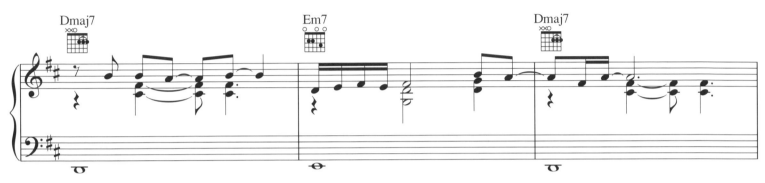

Tell me ___

just what you want me ___ to be. ___
what - ev - er you make it ___ to be. ___

One kiss ___ and boom, you're the on - ly one ___ for me. ___
Sun - shine ___ set on this cold lone - ly sea. ___

So please tell me why _____ don't you come a - round __
So please ba - by try _____ and use me for what __
why _____ don't you come a - round __

___ no more? _____ 'Cause right now I'm cry -
___ I'm good ___ for. _____ It ain't say - in' good - bye _____
___ no more? _____ 'Cause right now I'm dy -

in the game of love. It's all in this game of love.

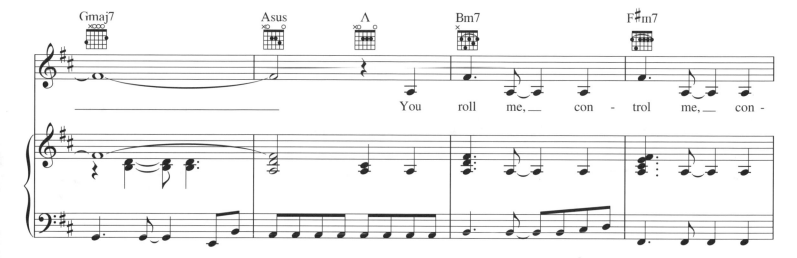

You roll me, con-trol me, con-

sole me. Please hold me. You guide me, di-

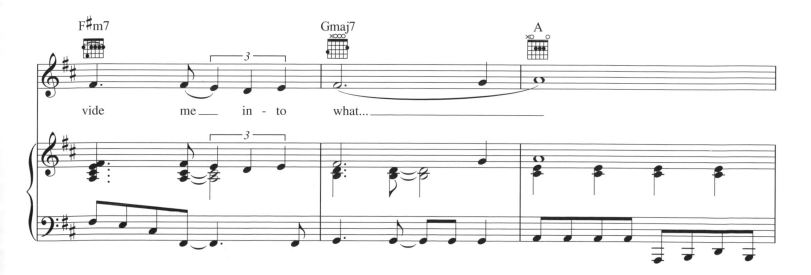

vide me in-to what...

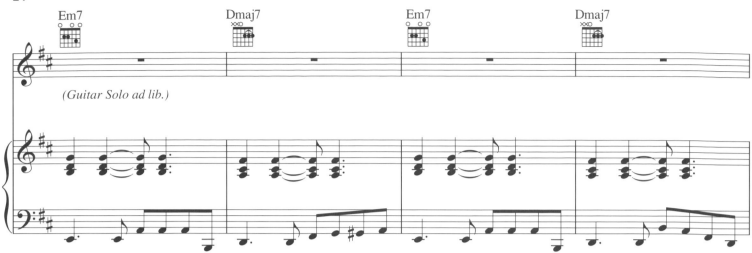

(Guitar Solo ad lib.)

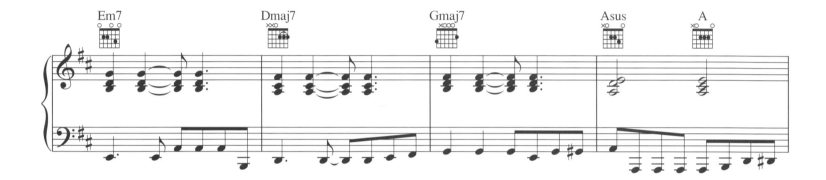

(Make ___ me feel good, yeah.)

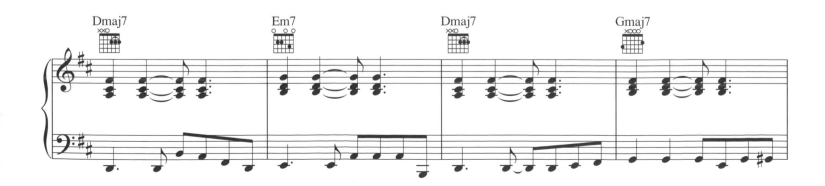

HEAVEN IS A PLACE ON EARTH

Words and Music by RICK NOWELS
and ELLEN SHIPLEY

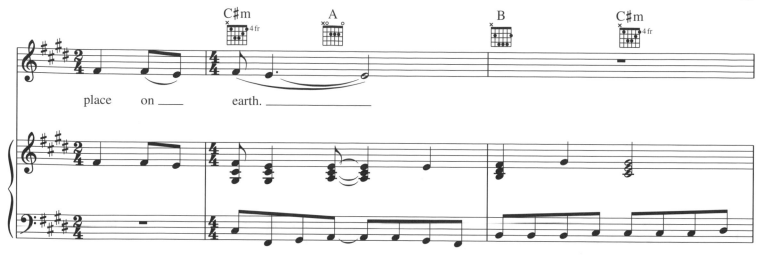

place on ___ earth. _____

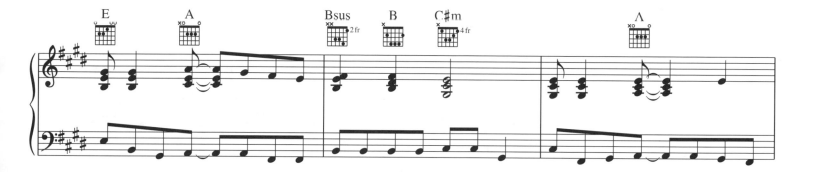

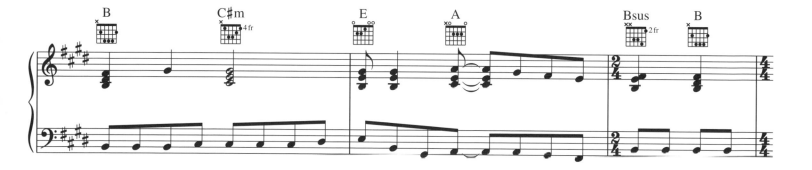

When the night falls _____
feel a —

down. ____ I wait for you ___ and you come a - round. ___ And the
lone, ___ I reach for you ___ and you bring me home. _ When I'm

world's a - live ___ with the sound of kids ___ on the
lost at _____ sea, ___ I hear your voice _ and it

street out - side. _ (1.) When you walk in - to the room, _____
car - ries me. __ (2., D.S.) In this world we're just be - gin - ning _

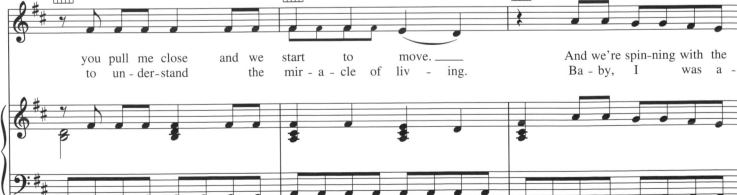

you pull me close and we start to move. _____ And we're spin-ning with the
to un - der - stand the mir - a - cle of liv - ing. Ba - by, I was a-

place on ___ earth. ___ When I

Ooh, heav - en is a place on ___ earth. ___

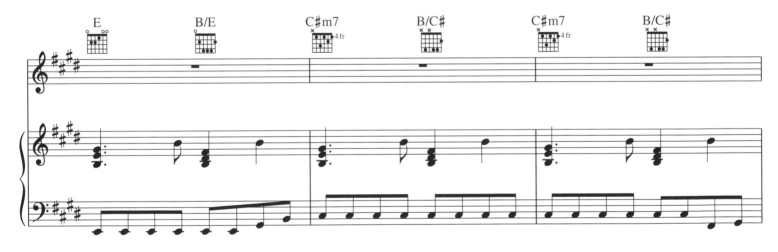

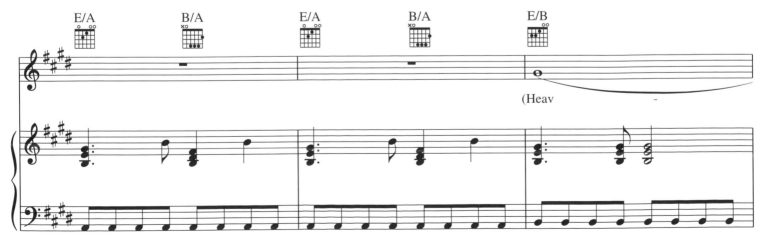

(Heav -

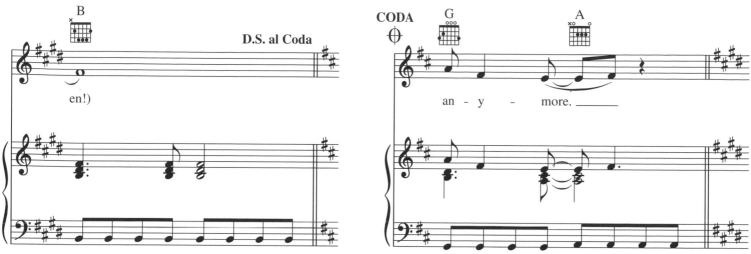

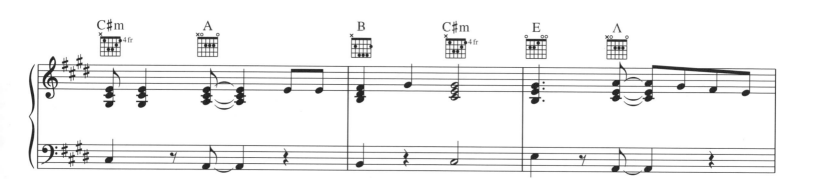

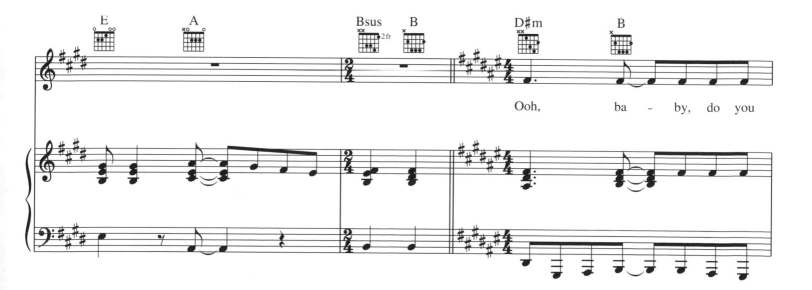

I DRIVE MYSELF CRAZY

Words and Music by RICK NOWELS,
ELLEN SHIPLEY and ALAN RICH

Moderately slow

I TURN TO YOU

Words and Music by MELANIE CHISHOLM,
RICK NOWELS and BILLY STEINBERG

Moderate Dance groove

Original key: E♭ minor. This edition has been transposed up one half-step to be more playable.

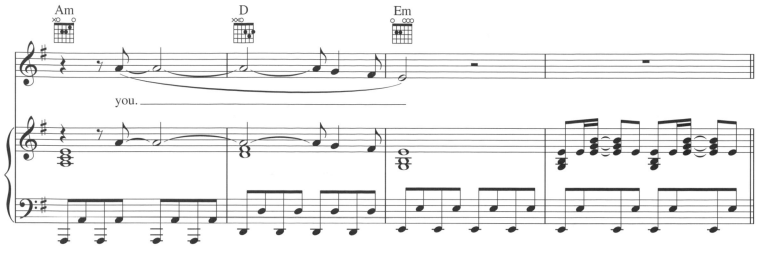

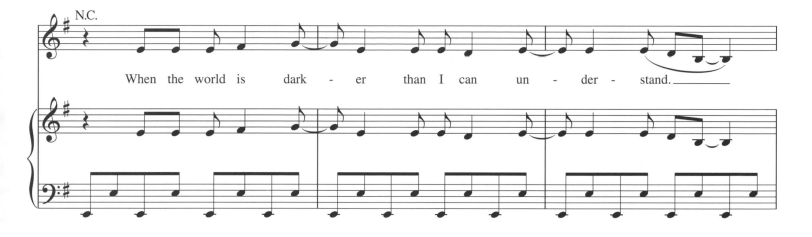

you.

When the world is dark - er than I can un - der - stand.

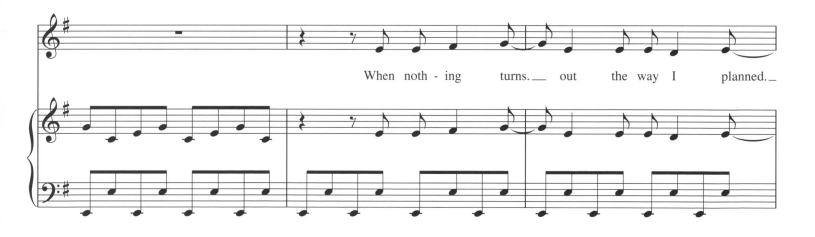

When noth - ing turns.__ out the way I planned.__

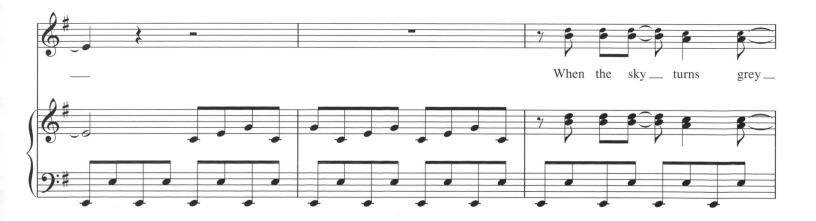

When the sky __ turns grey __

and there's no end in sight.

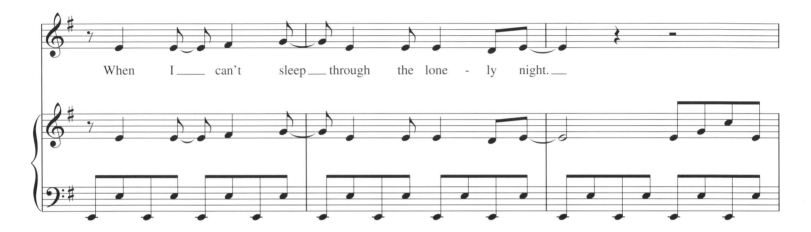

When I can't sleep through the lone - ly night.

I turn to you like a flow - er lean - ing to -

wards the sun. I turn to you 'cause

you're the on - ly one _____ who can turn _ me a -

round _ when I'm up - side down _

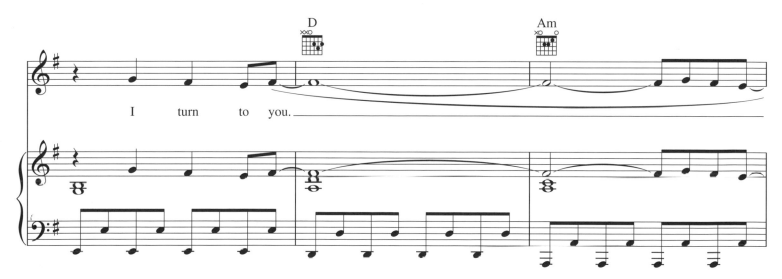

I turn to you. _____

To Coda ⊕

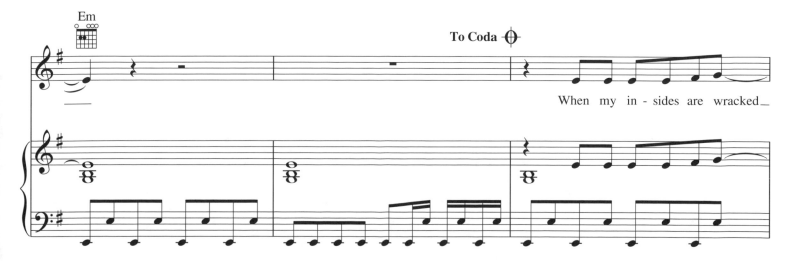

_ When my in - sides are wracked _

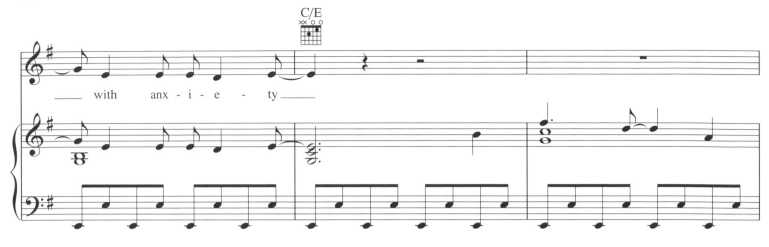

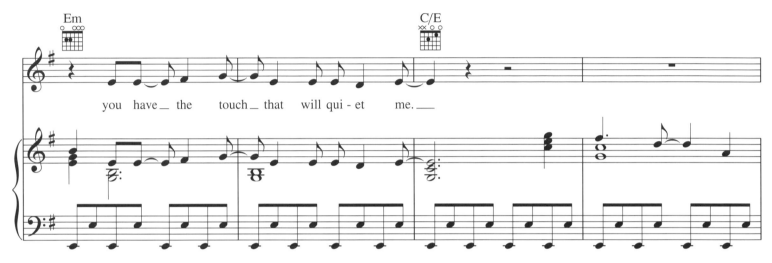

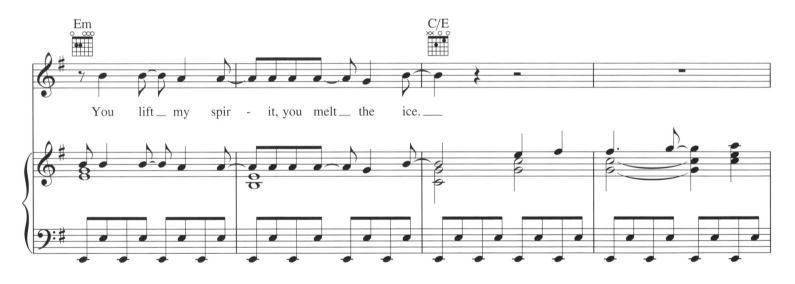

Where_ would I be? What_

would I do if you nev - er helped me through?_

_ I hope_

some - day if you've lost_ your way_ you could turn._

to me, (you could turn to me) like I turn to you.

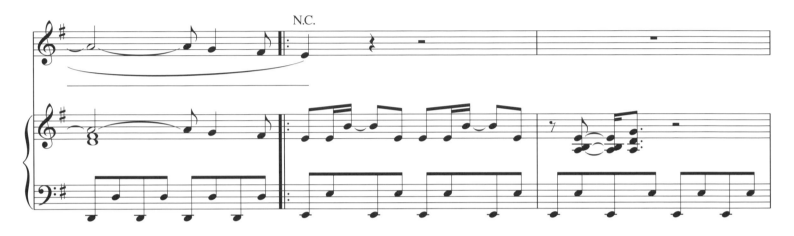

N.C.

1   2

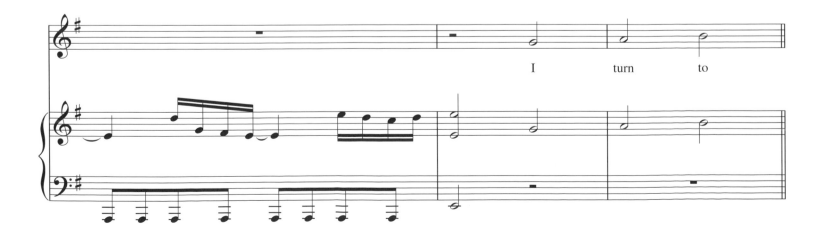

I turn to

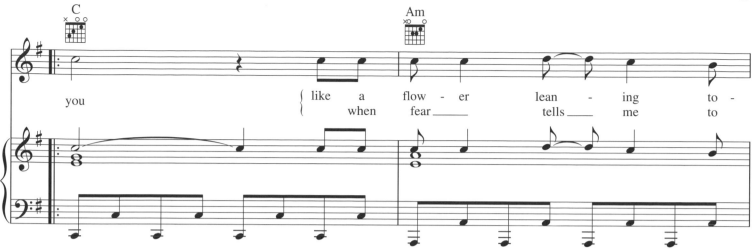

you
like a flow-er lean-ing to
when fear _____ tells _____ me to

wards the sun. _____
turn a - round. _____

I turn to you _____

'cause

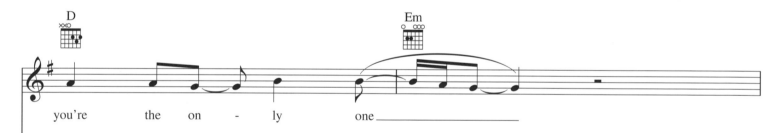

you're the on - ly one _____

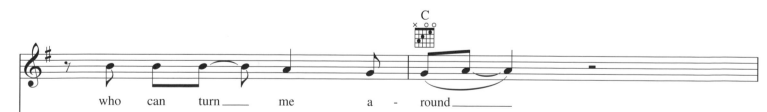

who can turn _____ me a - round _____

when I'm up - side down._____ I turn to you.__

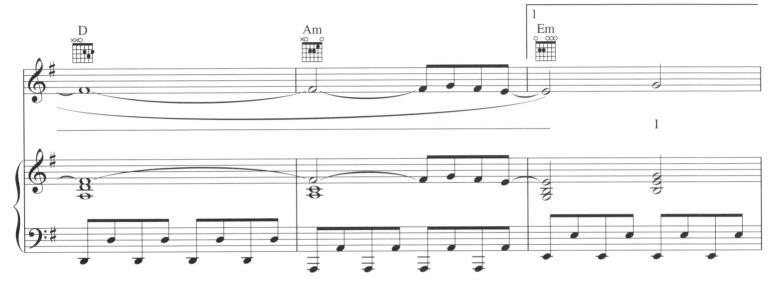

turn to

I

turn to ____ I turn to you.__

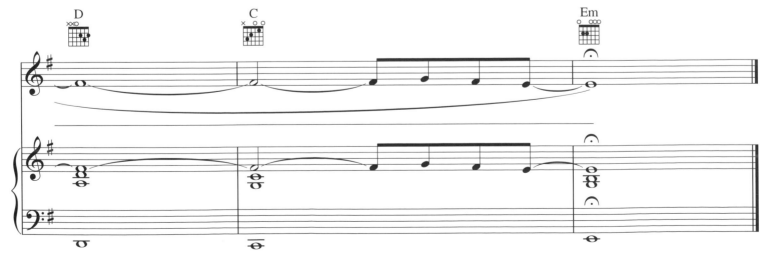

ONE AND ONE

Words and Music by RICK NOWELS,
BILLY STEINBERG and MARIE CLAIRE D'UBALDO

Moderate Dance beat

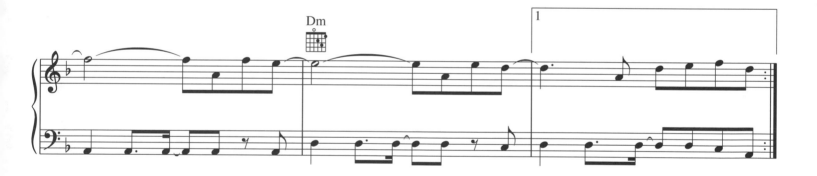

The sky is-n't al - ways blue. _____

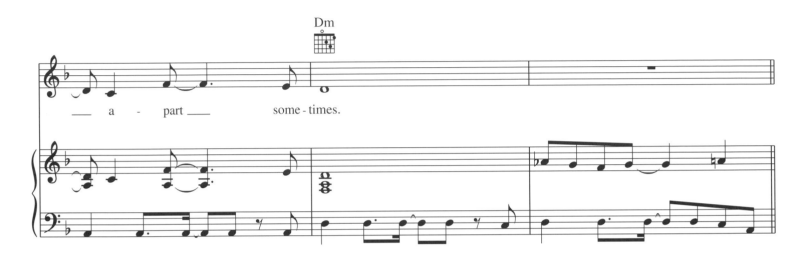

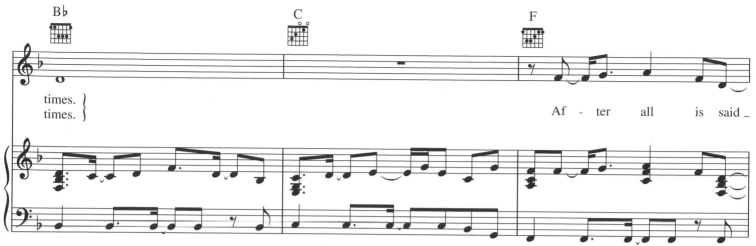

times.
times.

After all is said

and done,   one and one   still is one.

When we cry,   when we laugh,   I am half,

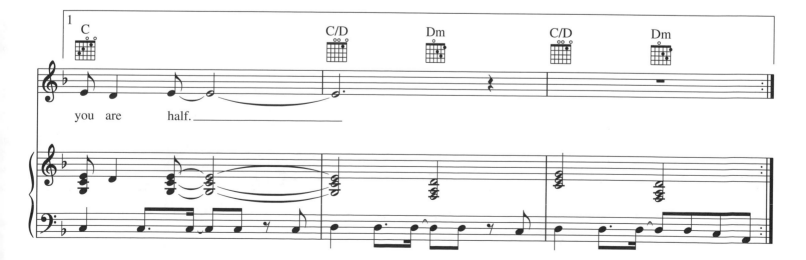

you are half.

you are half. Look how far we have come.

One and one still is... One moon, (one

moon,) one star, (one star,) I love the one we are.

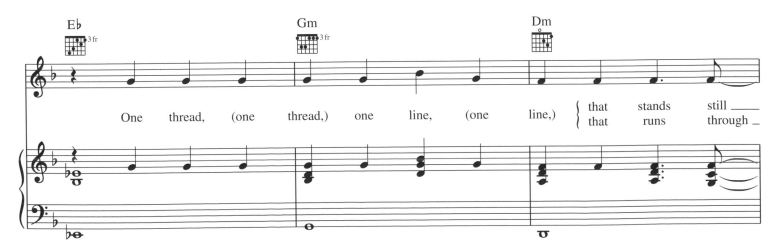

One thread, (one thread,) one line, (one line,) { that stands still / that runs through

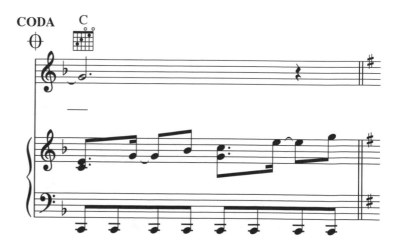

After all is said ___ and done, one ___ and one still ___

___ is one. When ___ we cry, when ___ we laugh,

I ___ am half, you ___ are half. Look ___ how far we ___

___ have come. One ___ and one still ___ is one.

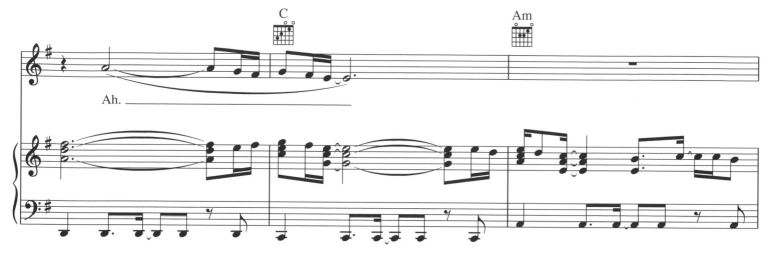

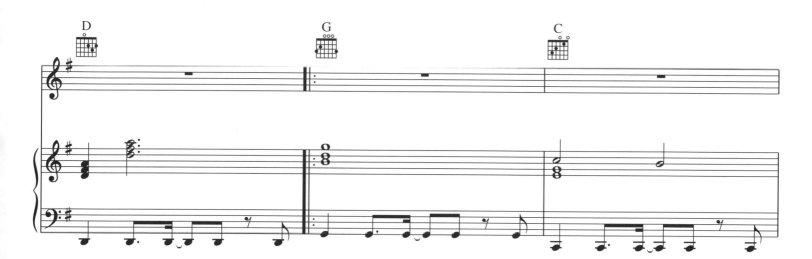

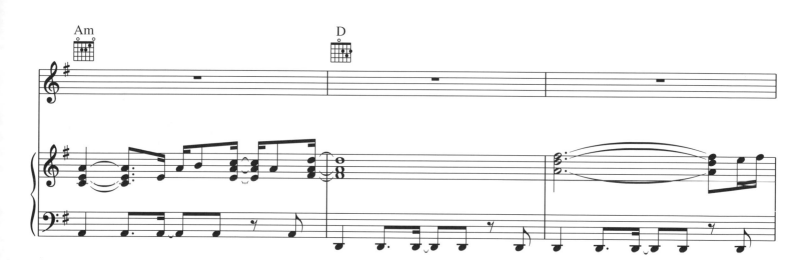

THE POWER OF GOODBYE

Words and Music by RICK NOWELS
and MADONNA

Moderately steady beat

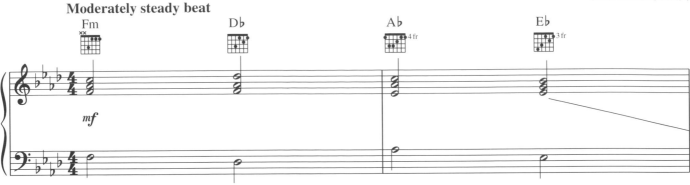

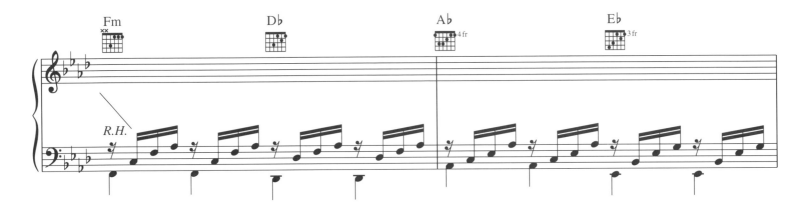

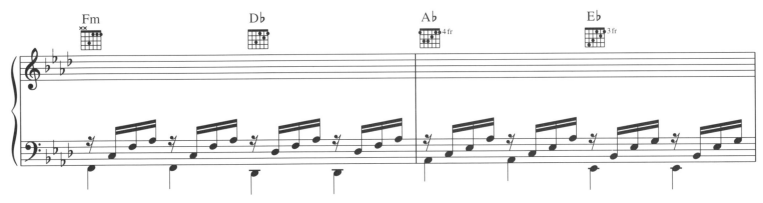

Your heart is not

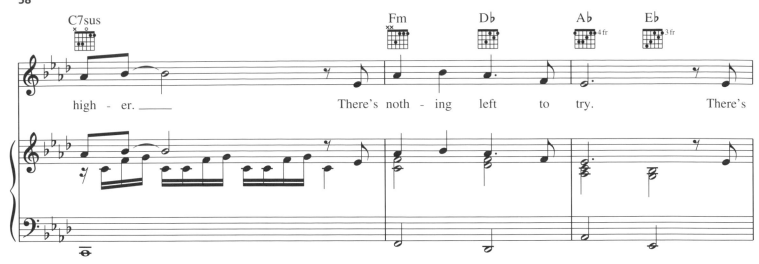

high - er. _____ There's noth - ing left to try. There's

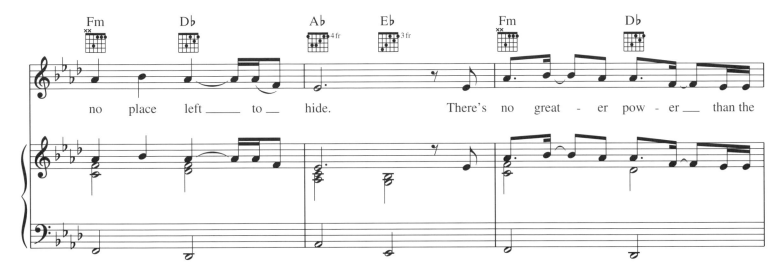

no place left _____ to _ hide. There's no great - er pow - er _____ than the

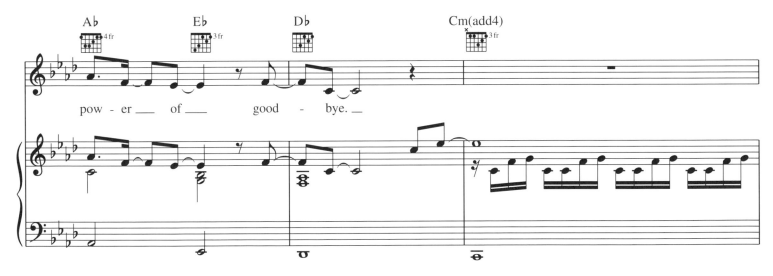

pow - er _____ of _____ good - bye. _____

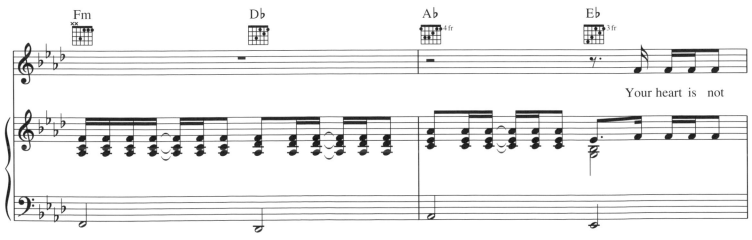

Your heart is not

o - pen, so I must go. The spell has been ___ bro - ken. I loved you ___

Instrumental solo

___ so. ___ You were my les - son I had to

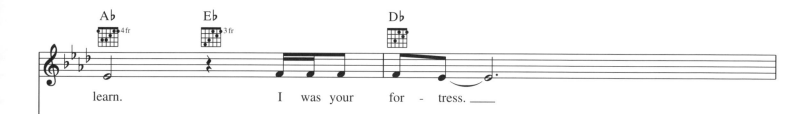

learn. I was your for - tress. ___

Solo ends

There's noth - ing left to
There's noth - ing left to

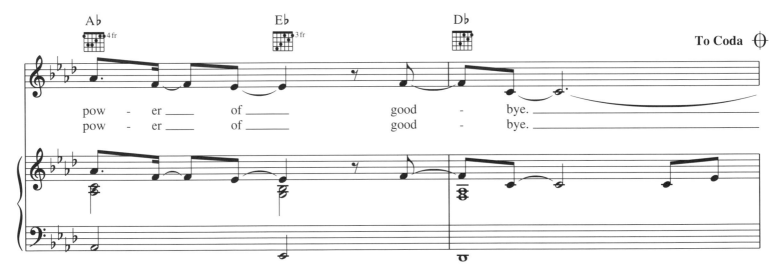

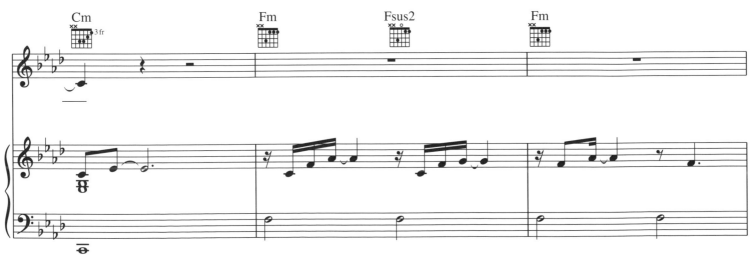

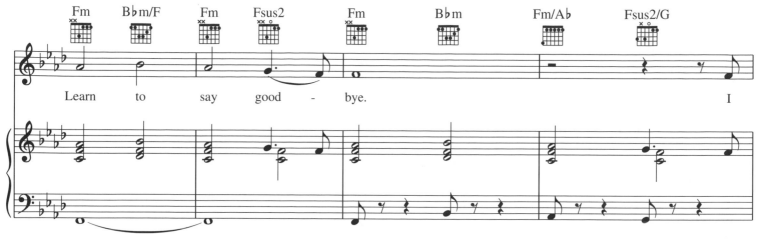

Learn to say good-bye.
I

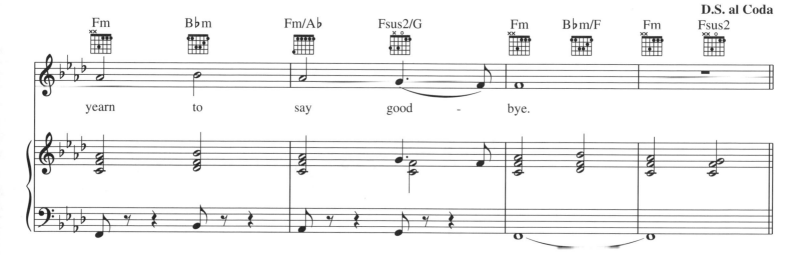

yearn to say good-bye.

D.S. al Coda

CODA

There's noth-ing left to

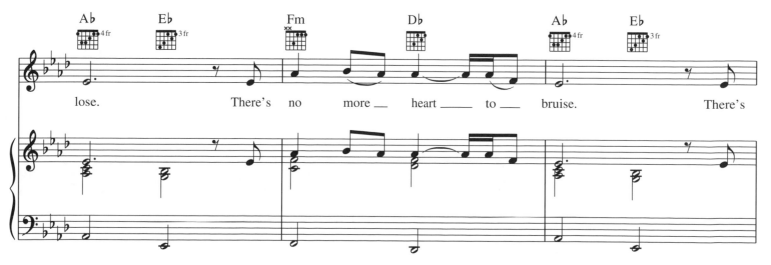

lose. There's no more heart to bruise. There's

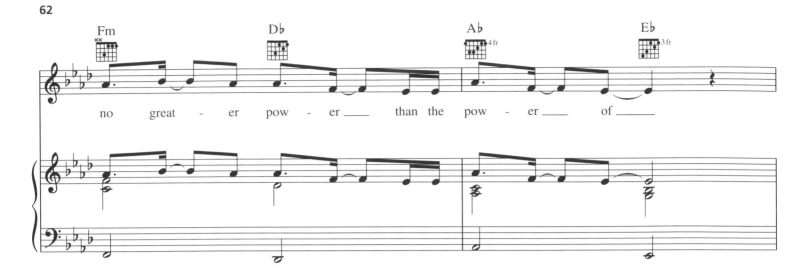

no great - er pow - er _____ than the pow - er _____ of _____

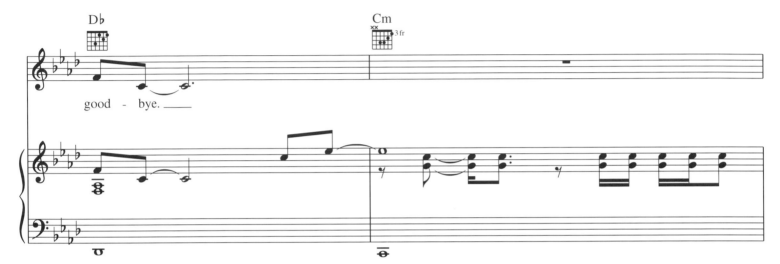

good - bye. _____

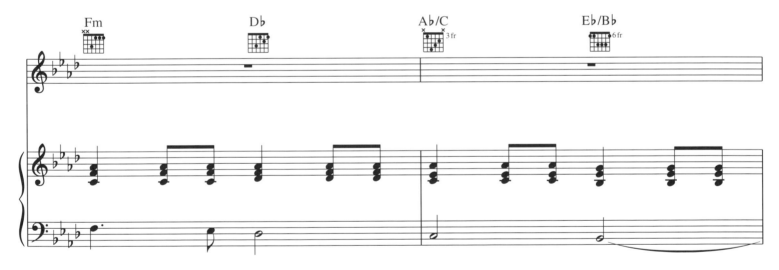

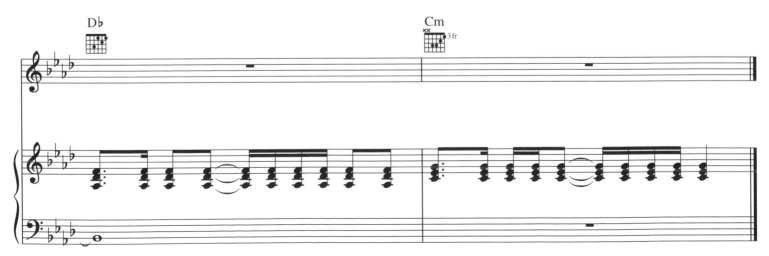

ROOMS ON FIRE

Words and Music by STEVIE NICKS
and RICK NOWELS

It seems like it was the cre - a - tion of some of those
that she could sense for miles._____ She

same old things._____ It seemed to be the on - ly thing_
dreamed of her wan - ton lux - ur - y.____ And she laughed and she cried and she

_____ left out in the light._____
tried to in the taunt_ him._____

She had trust - ed man - y but been
And he hat - ed _____ to be

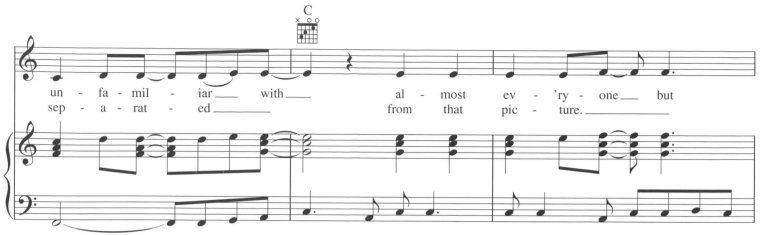

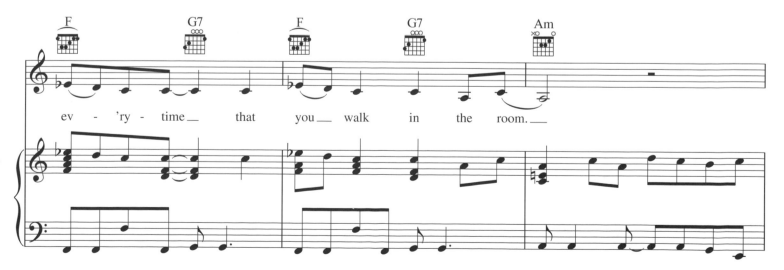

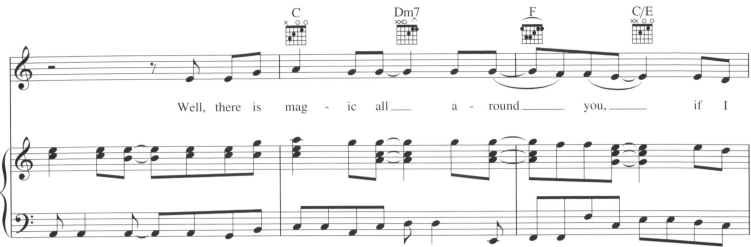

Well, there is mag - ic all ___ a - round ___ you, ___ if I

do say so my - self, ___ I have ___ known ___ this much

long - er than I've known you. ___

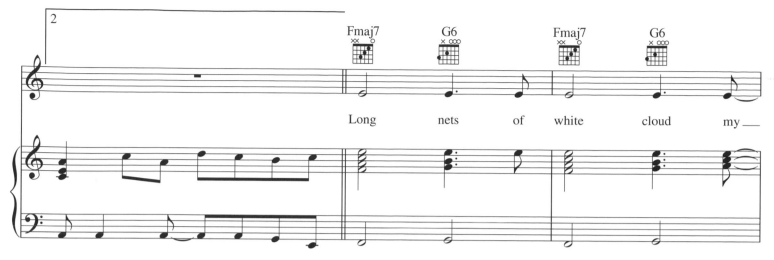

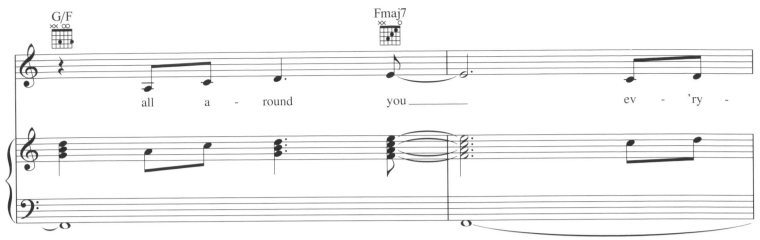

all a - round you _____ ev - 'ry -

time you walk in the room. _____ Well,

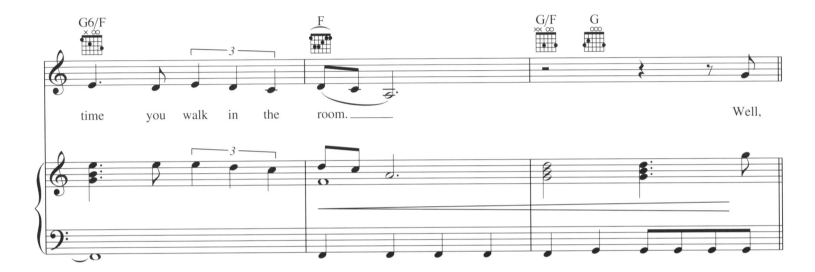

may - be I'm _____ just think - ing that the rooms _____

_____ are all _____ on fire, _____

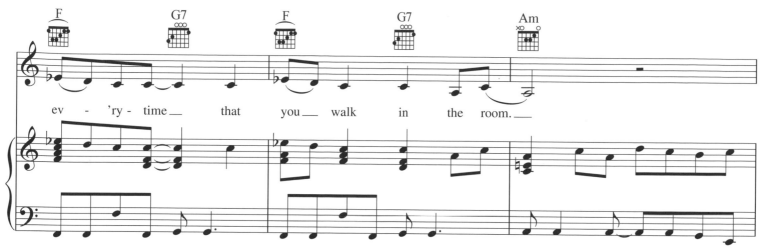

ev - 'ry - time___ that you___ walk in the room.___

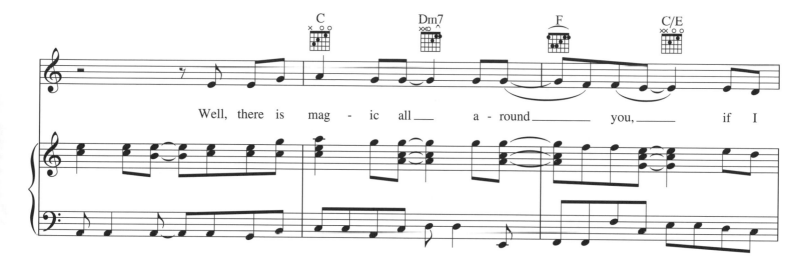

Well, there is mag - ic all___ a - round___ you,___ if I

do say so my - self,___ Well, I have___ known_ this much

Repeat and Fade

long - er than I've known you.___

Well,

SEXUAL
(Li Da Di)

Words and Music by RICK NOWELS,
MARIE-CLAIRE CREMERS and BILLY STEINBERG

Hey! ___ Don't make ___ this one ___ di - men -

tion - al. The way I feel ___ is sex - u - al. The

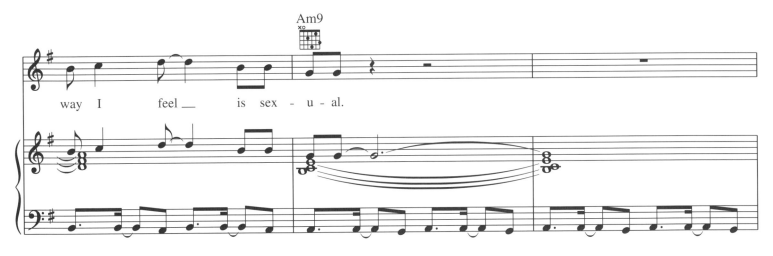

way I feel ___ is sex - u - al.

It can't ___ just be ___ in - tel - lec - tu - al. The

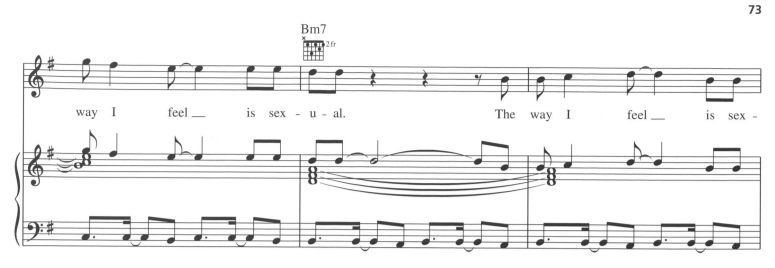

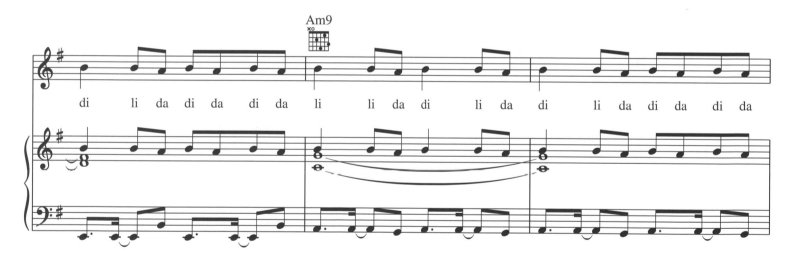

di li da di da di da.) I con - fess _____ I _____ watch your

mouth move _ ba - by _____ when you're speak - ing. (Di li da

di li da di.) Stud - y _____ your _____ bod - y

when you _ walk _____ out _____ of the room. (Li da di li da

di li da di.) You'll _ see ___ how much _ you ___ val - ue my friend -

- ship, ___ hey! ___ But I want you ad - dict - ed ___

D.S. al Coda

to my ___ per - fume. _ Hey! _

me.
(Li li da di li da di li da di da di da

li li da di li da.) When you're next to _____ me. _____ (Li li da di li da

di li da di da di da li li da di li da di li da di da di da.)

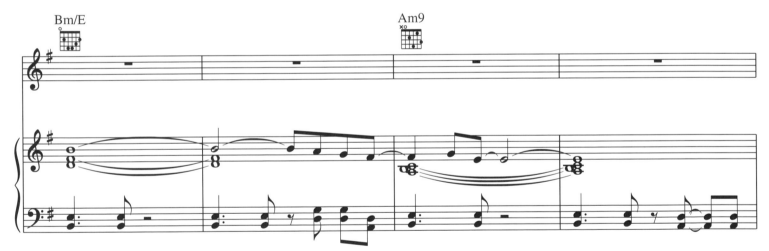

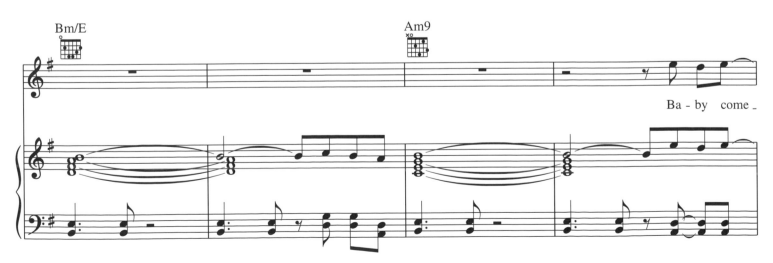

Ba - by come

_____ to me _____ and let me kiss _____ you, _____ oh. _

_____ Let me show _____ you the things. _____ I _____ can do _

_____ for _____ you. _ Hey! _ Don't make _

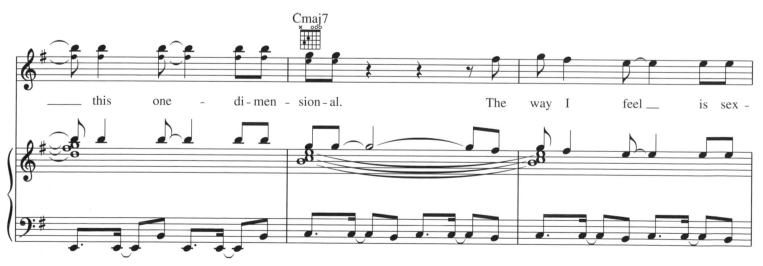

_____ this one - di - men - sion - al. The way I feel _ is sex -

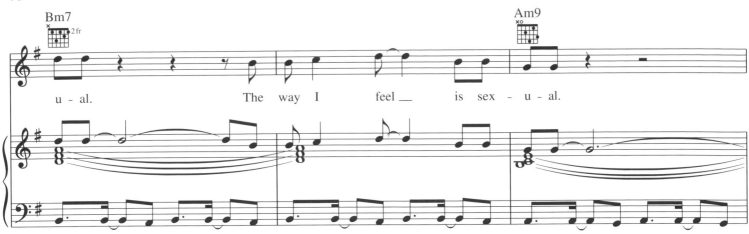

u - al. The way I feel __ is sex - u - al.

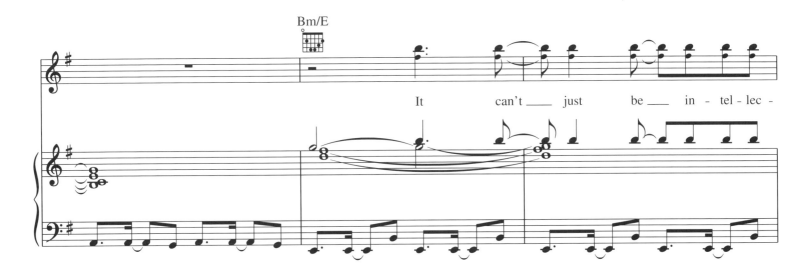

It can't __ just be __ in - tel - lec -

tu - al. The way I feel __ is sex - u - al. The

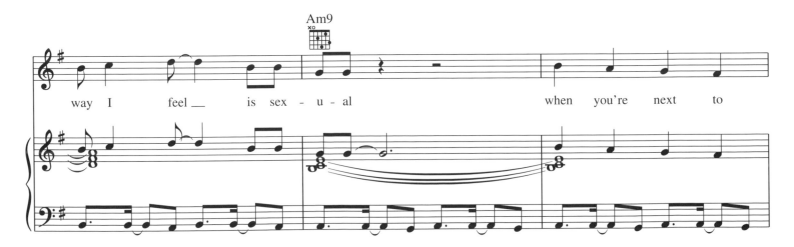

way I feel __ is sex - u - al when you're next to

(Li li da di li da di li da di da di da li li da di li da.)

When you're next to me. _____
(Li li da di li da di li da di da di da

Repeat and Fade

li li da di li da di li da di da di da.) (Li li da di li da

Optional Ending

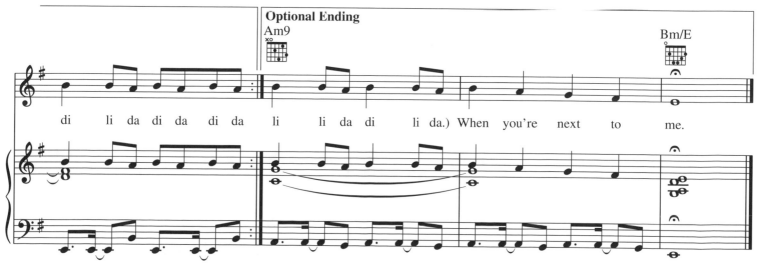

di li da di da di da li li da di li da.) When you're next to me.

YOU GET WHAT YOU GIVE

Words and Music by GREGG ALEXANDER
and RICK NOWELS

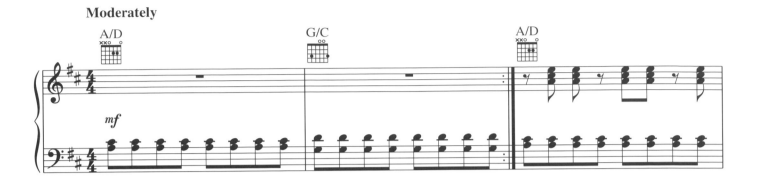

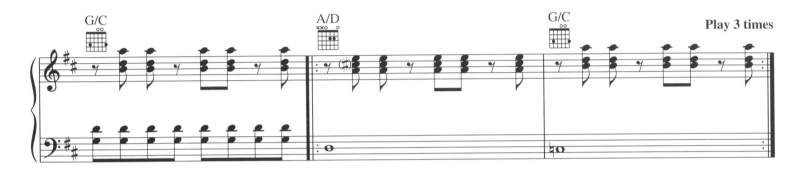

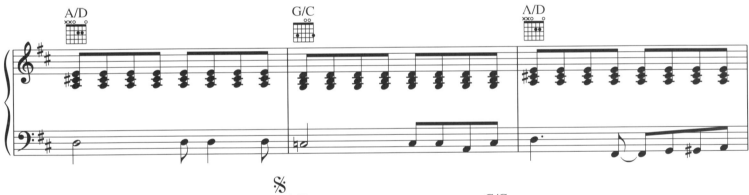

Wake   up,   kids. __ We've got   the dream-ers dis - ease. __
Frien - e - mies, __ who when you're down ain't your   friend. __
Four   A.   M., __ we ran   a mir - a - cle   mile. __

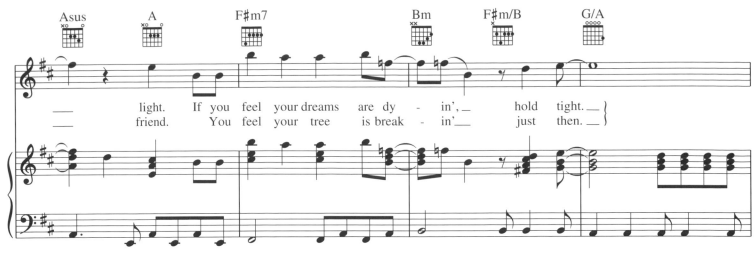

light. If you feel your dreams are dy - in', __ hold tight. __

friend. You feel your tree is break - in' __ just then. __

You've got the mu - sic in you. __ Don't let go. You've got the mu - sic in you. __

__ One dance left. This world is gon - na pull through. _ Don't give up.

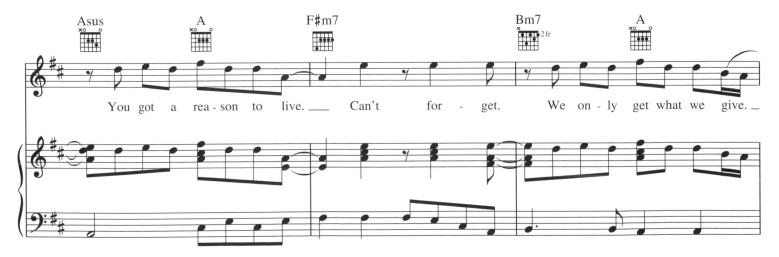

You got a rea - son to live. __ Can't for - get. We on - ly get what we give. _

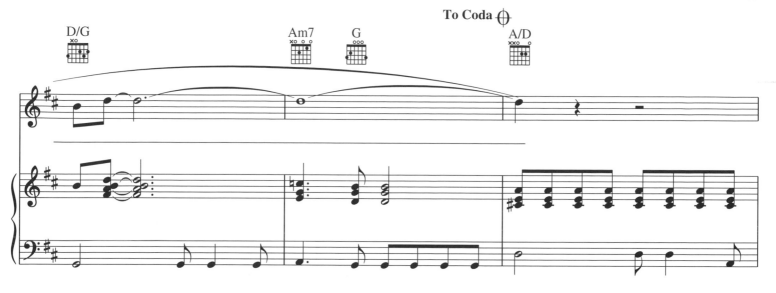

I'm com-in' home, ba - by.   You're   tops.   Give it to me now.

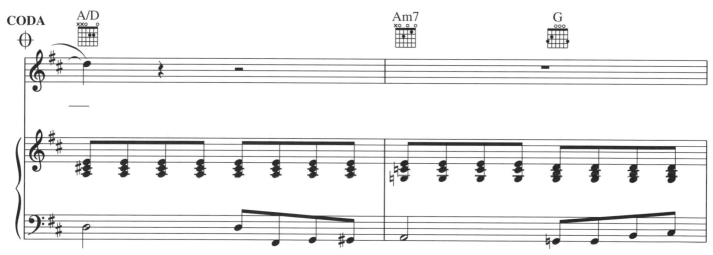

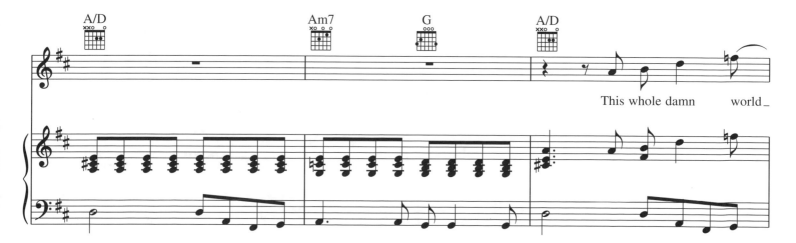

This whole damn   world

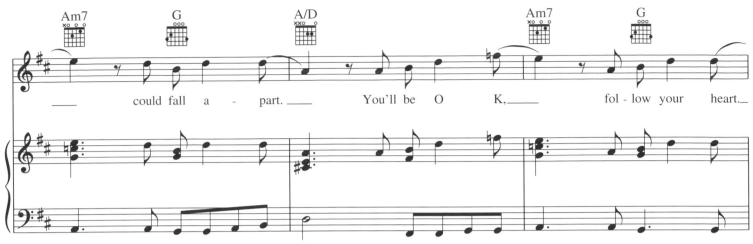

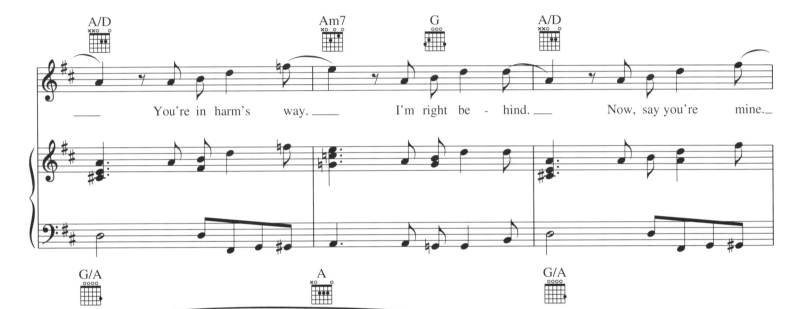

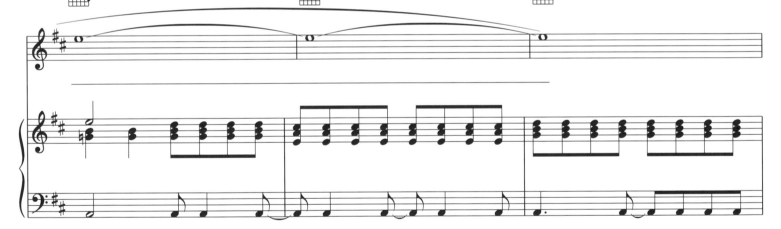

One dance left. This world is gon-na pull through.___ Don't give up.

You've got a rea-son to live. ___ Can't for - get. We on - ly get what we give.___

___ Don't let go. I feel the mu-sic in you, ___ yo, hey, hey,

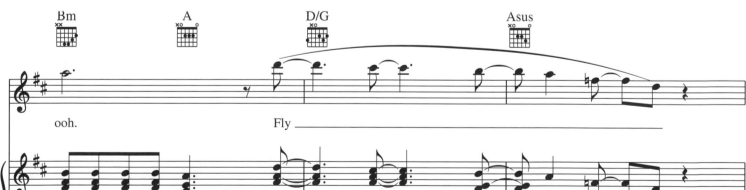

ooh.   Fly ___

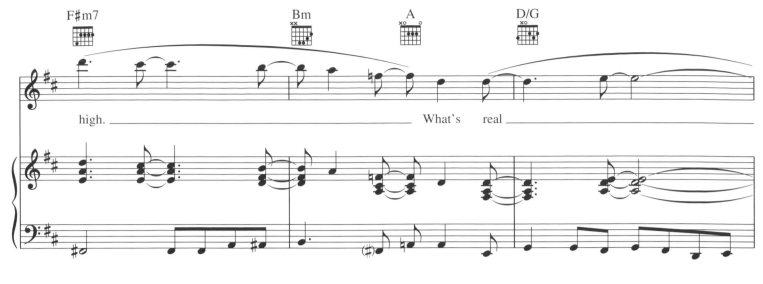

high. _____ What's real _____

___ can't die. _____

_____ You on - ly get what you give. ___

You're gon - na get what you give. ___ Don't give up. Just don't be a - fraid to leave. _

Health in - sur - ance rip off ly - ing,
Fash - ion shoots with Beck and Han - son,

F. D. A., big bank - ers buy - ing. Fake com - put - er crash - es din - ing, clon - ing while they're mul - ti - ply - ing.
Court - ney Love and Mar - 'lyn Man - son. You're all fakes, run to your man - sions.

Come a - round, we'll kick your ass in.   Don't   let   go.
                                                Don't   give   up.

One   dance   left.
Can't   for - get.

STANDING STILL

Words and Music by RICK NOWELS
and JEWEL KILCHER

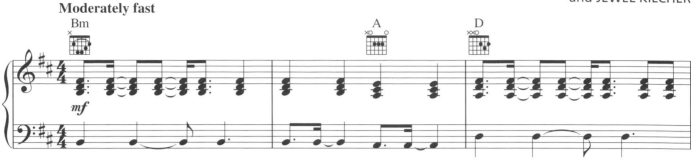

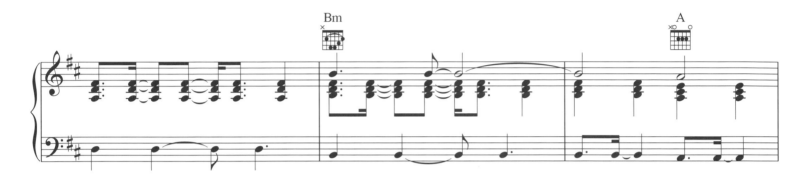

Cut - tin' through ___ the
Moth - ers on the stoop, boys in

dark - est night ___ in my two head - lights. ___

Tryin' to

souped - up coupes ___ on this hot sum - mer night. ___

Be - tween

keep it clear,___ but I'm los-ing it here___ to the twi-light.___
fight and___ flight is the blind___ man's___ sight and the choice that's right.___

There's a dead end to my left; there's a burn-ing bush___
I roll the win-dow down, feel like I'm gon-na drown___ in

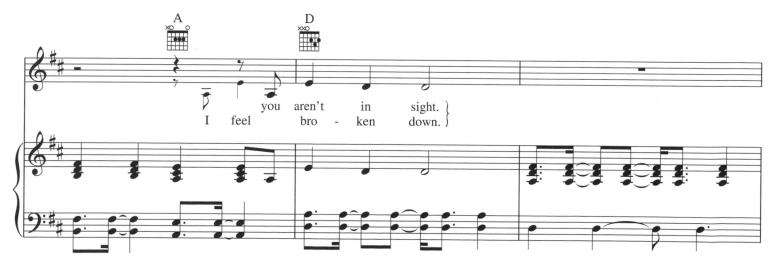

to my right.___ You___ aren't in sight;
this strange town.___ Feel___ bro-ken down;

you aren't in sight.
I feel bro-ken down.

Do you {want need} me

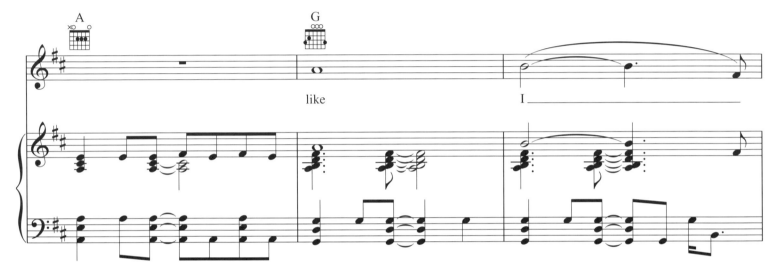

like I

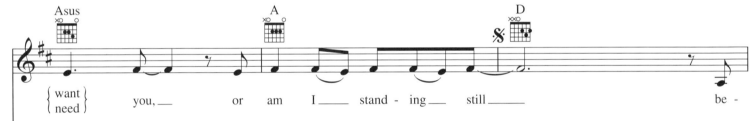

{want need} you, or am I stand-ing still be-

neath the dark-ened sky? Or am I stand-ing still

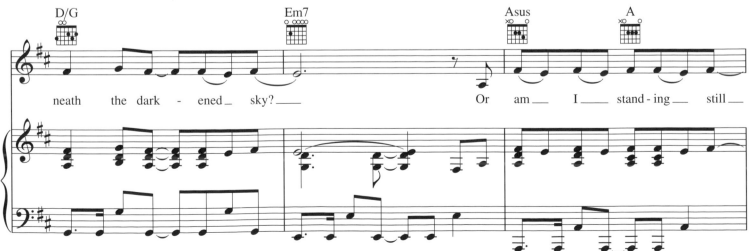

with the scen - er - y fly - ing— by?— Or

am— I— stand - ing still?———— Out of the cor - ner of— my— eye,—

— was that you

pass - ing me— by?——————————

CODA

Are you pass- - - - - - - - - ing me

by, pass - ing___ by?___

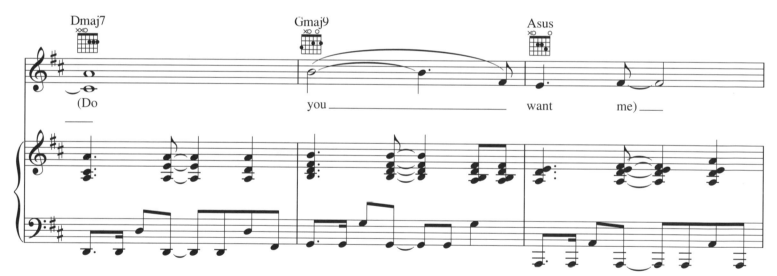

(Do you_____ want me)___

Pass - ing me by. Do you___ need me___

like I _____ need you too? _ And do you _

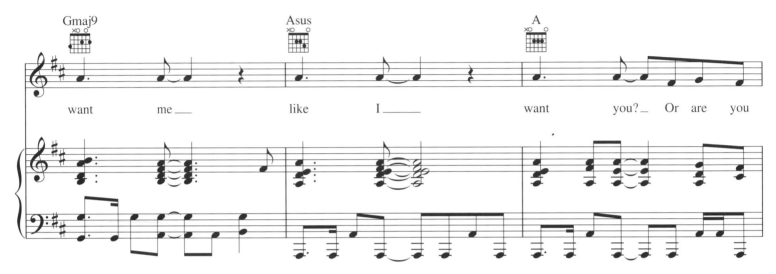

want me _ like I _____ want you? _ Or are you

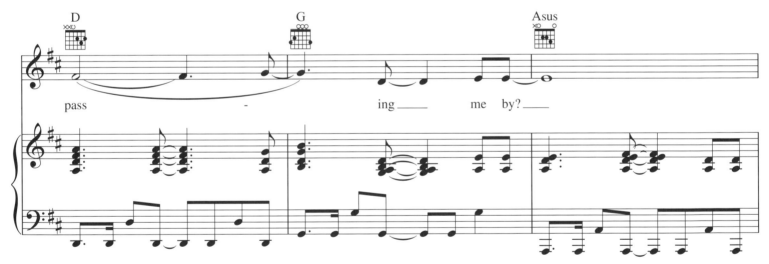

pass - ing _ me by? _

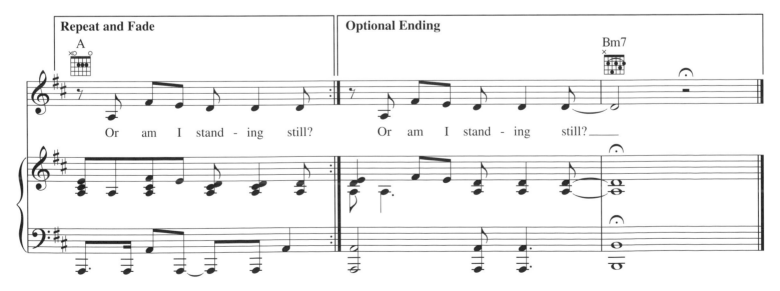

Repeat and Fade

Or am I stand - ing still?

Optional Ending

Or am I stand - ing still? _____